GOOD DAY START WITH
GRATITUDE

THIS JOURNAL BELONGS TO :

____

GRATITUDE

TODAY'S AFFIRMATION   /   /

"

"

3 THINGS I'LL ACCOMPLISH TODAY   3 THINGS I LOOK FORWARD TO

1.   1.

2.   2.

3.   3.

TO DAY'S SCHEDULE

WHAT WOULD MAKE TO DAY GREAT?

HOW CAN I SET MYSELF FOR SUCCESS TO DAY?

HOW DO I WANT TO FEEL AT THE END OF TODAY?

TODAY'S AFFIRMATION   /   /

"

"

3 THINGS I'LL ACCOMPLISH TODAY

1.

2.

3.

3 THINGS I LOOK FORWARD TO

1.

2.

3.

TO DAY'S SCHEDULE

- [ ]
- [ ]
- [ ]
- [ ]
- [ ]
- [ ]
- [ ]

WHAT WOULD MAKE TO DAY GREAT?

HOW CAN I SET MYSELF FOR SUCCESS TO DAY?

HOW DO I WANT TO FEEL AT THE END OF TODAY?

GRATITUDE

TODAY'S AFFIRMATION   /   /

"

"

3 THINGS I'LL ACCOMPLISH TODAY

1.

2.

3.

3 THINGS I LOOK FORWARD TO

1.

2.

3.

TO DAY'S SCHEDULE

WHAT WOULD MAKE TO DAY GREAT?

HOW CAN I SET MYSELF FOR SUCCESS TO DAY?

HOW DO I WANT TO FEEL AT THE END OF TODAY?

SHARE YOUR JOY

TODAY'S AFFIRMATION   /   /

"

"

3 THINGS I'LL ACCOMPLISH TODAY   3 THINGS I LOOK FORWARD TO

1.   1.

2.   2.

3.   3.

TO DAY'S SCHEDULE

☐
☐
☐
☐
☐
☐
☐

WHAT WOULD MAKE TO DAY GREAT?

HOW CAN I SET MYSELF FOR SUCCESS TO DAY?

HOW DO I WANT TO FEEL AT THE END OF TODAY?

TODAY'S AFFIRMATION   /   /

"

"

3 THINGS I'LL ACCOMPLISH TODAY   3 THINGS I LOOK FORWARD TO

1.   1.

2.   2.

3.   3.

TO DAY'S SCHEDULE

WHAT WOULD MAKE TO DAY GREAT?

HOW CAN I SET MYSELF FOR SUCCESS TO DAY?

HOW DO I WANT TO FEEL AT THE END OF TODAY?

TODAY'S AFFIRMATION   /   /

"

"

3 THINGS I'LL ACCOMPLISH TODAY   3 THINGS I LOOK FORWARD TO

1.   1.

2.   2.

3.   3.

TO DAY'S SCHEDULE

☐
☐
☐
☐
☐
☐
☐

WHAT WOULD MAKE TO DAY GREAT?

HOW CAN I SET MYSELF FOR SUCCESS TO DAY?

HOW DO I WANT TO FEEL AT THE END OF TODAY?

TODAY'S AFFIRMATION   /   /

"

"

3 THINGS I'LL ACCOMPLISH TODAY   3 THINGS I LOOK FORWARD TO

1.   1.

2.   2.

3.   3.

TO DAY'S SCHEDULE

WHAT WOULD MAKE TO DAY GREAT?

HOW CAN I SET MYSELF FOR SUCCESS TO DAY?

HOW DO I WANT TO FEEL AT THE END OF TODAY?

TODAY'S AFFIRMATION   /   /

"

"

3 THINGS I'LL ACCOMPLISH TODAY

1.

2.

3.

3 THINGS I LOOK FORWARD TO

1.

2.

3.

TO DAY'S SCHEDULE

☐
☐
☐
☐
☐
☐
☐

WHAT WOULD MAKE TO DAY GREAT?

HOW CAN I SET MYSELF FOR SUCCESS TO DAY?

HOW DO I WANT TO FEEL AT THE END OF TODAY?

SHARE YOUR JOY

GRATITUDE

TODAY'S AFFIRMATION   /   /

"

"

3 THINGS I'LL ACCOMPLISH TODAY

1.

2.

3.

3 THINGS I LOOK FORWARD TO

1.

2.

3.

TO DAY'S SCHEDULE

WHAT WOULD MAKE TO DAY GREAT?

HOW CAN I SET MYSELF FOR SUCCESS TO DAY?

HOW DO I WANT TO FEEL AT THE END OF TODAY?

GRATITUDE

TODAY'S AFFIRMATION   /   /

"

"

3 THINGS I'LL ACCOMPLISH TODAY

1.

2.

3.

3 THINGS I LOOK FORWARD TO

1.

2.

3.

TO DAY'S SCHEDULE

- [ ]
- [ ]
- [ ]
- [ ]
- [ ]
- [ ]

WHAT WOULD MAKE TO DAY GREAT?

HOW CAN I SET MYSELF FOR SUCCESS TO DAY?

HOW DO I WANT TO FEEL AT THE END OF TODAY?

GRATITUDE

TODAY'S AFFIRMATION   /   /

"

"

3 THINGS I'LL ACCOMPLISH TODAY

1.

2.

3.

3 THINGS I LOOK FORWARD TO

1.

2.

3.

TO DAY'S SCHEDULE

☐
☐
☐
☐
☐
☐
☐

WHAT WOULD MAKE TO DAY GREAT?

HOW CAN I SET MYSELF FOR SUCCESS TO DAY?

HOW DO I WANT TO FEEL AT THE END OF TODAY?

GRATITUDE

TODAY'S AFFIRMATION   /   /

"

"

3 THINGS I'LL ACCOMPLISH TODAY

1.

2.

3.

3 THINGS I LOOK FORWARD TO

1.

2.

3.

TO DAY'S SCHEDULE

☐
☐
☐
☐
☐
☐
☐

WHAT WOULD MAKE TO DAY GREAT?

HOW CAN I SET MYSELF FOR SUCCESS TO DAY?

HOW DO I WANT TO FEEL AT THE END OF TODAY?

TODAY'S AFFIRMATION   /   /

"

"

3 THINGS I'LL ACCOMPLISH TODAY

1.

2.

3.

3 THINGS I LOOK FORWARD TO

1.

2.

3.

TO DAY'S SCHEDULE

WHAT WOULD MAKE TO DAY GREAT?

HOW CAN I SET MYSELF FOR SUCCESS TO DAY?

HOW DO I WANT TO FEEL AT THE END OF TODAY?

GRATITUDE

TODAY'S AFFIRMATION   /   /

"

"

3 THINGS I'LL ACCOMPLISH TODAY

1.

2.

3.

3 THINGS I LOOK FORWARD TO

1.

2.

3.

TO DAY'S SCHEDULE

☐

☐

☐

☐

☐

☐

WHAT WOULD MAKE TO DAY GREAT?

HOW CAN I SET MYSELF FOR SUCCESS TO DAY?

HOW DO I WANT TO FEEL AT THE END OF TODAY?

GRATITUDE

TODAY'S AFFIRMATION   /   /

"

"

3 THINGS I'LL ACCOMPLISH TODAY

1.

2.

3.

3 THINGS I LOOK FORWARD TO

1.

2.

3.

TO DAY'S SCHEDULE

WHAT WOULD MAKE TO DAY GREAT?

HOW CAN I SET MYSELF FOR SUCCESS TO DAY?

HOW DO I WANT TO FEEL AT THE END OF TODAY?

TODAY'S AFFIRMATION   /   /

"

"

3 THINGS I'LL ACCOMPLISH TODAY   3 THINGS I LOOK FORWARD TO

1.   1.

2.   2.

3.   3.

TO DAY'S SCHEDULE

☐
☐
☐
☐
☐
☐
☐

WHAT WOULD MAKE TO DAY GREAT?

HOW CAN I SET MYSELF FOR SUCCESS TO DAY?

HOW DO I WANT TO FEEL AT THE END OF TODAY?

TODAY'S AFFIRMATION   /   /

"

"

3 THINGS I'LL ACCOMPLISH TODAY   3 THINGS I LOOK FORWARD TO

1.   1.

2.   2.

3.   3.

TO DAY'S SCHEDULE

WHAT WOULD MAKE TO DAY GREAT?

HOW CAN I SET MYSELF FOR SUCCESS TO DAY?

HOW DO I WANT TO FEEL AT THE END OF TODAY?

GRATITUDE

TODAY'S AFFIRMATION   /   /

"

"

3 THINGS I'LL ACCOMPLISH TODAY

1.

2.

3.

3 THINGS I LOOK FORWARD TO

1.

2.

3.

TO DAY'S SCHEDULE

- [ ]
- [ ]
- [ ]
- [ ]
- [ ]
- [ ]
- [ ]

WHAT WOULD MAKE TO DAY GREAT?

HOW CAN I SET MYSELF FOR SUCCESS TO DAY?

HOW DO I WANT TO FEEL AT THE END OF TODAY?

TODAY'S AFFIRMATION　　　　　　　　　　/　　　　　/

"

"

3 THINGS I'LL ACCOMPLISH TODAY

1.

2.

3.

3 THINGS I LOOK FORWARD TO

1.

2.

3.

TO DAY'S SCHEDULE

WHAT WOULD MAKE TO DAY GREAT?

HOW CAN I SET MYSELF FOR SUCCESS TO DAY?

HOW DO I WANT TO FEEL AT THE END OF TODAY?

TODAY'S AFFIRMATION   /   /

"

                                                                    "

3 THINGS I'LL ACCOMPLISH TODAY   3 THINGS I LOOK FORWARD TO

1.   1.

2.   2.

3.   3.

TO DAY'S SCHEDULE

- [ ]
- [ ]
- [ ]
- [ ]
- [ ]
- [ ]
- [ ]

WHAT WOULD MAKE TO DAY GREAT?

HOW CAN I SET MYSELF FOR SUCCESS TO DAY?

HOW DO I WANT TO FEEL AT THE END OF TODAY?

TODAY'S AFFIRMATION   /   /

"

"

3 THINGS I'LL ACCOMPLISH TODAY   3 THINGS I LOOK FORWARD TO

1.   1.

2.   2.

3.   3.

TO DAY'S SCHEDULE

WHAT WOULD MAKE TO DAY GREAT?

HOW CAN I SET MYSELF FOR SUCCESS TO DAY?

HOW DO I WANT TO FEEL AT THE END OF TODAY?

GRATITUDE

TODAY'S AFFIRMATION   /   /

"

"

3 THINGS I'LL ACCOMPLISH TODAY   3 THINGS I LOOK FORWARD TO

1.   1.

2.   2.

3.   3.

TO DAY'S SCHEDULE

☐
☐
☐
☐
☐
☐
☐

WHAT WOULD MAKE TO DAY GREAT?

HOW CAN I SET MYSELF FOR SUCCESS TO DAY?

HOW DO I WANT TO FEEL AT THE END OF TODAY?

TODAY'S AFFIRMATION   /   /

"

"

3 THINGS I'LL ACCOMPLISH TODAY   3 THINGS I LOOK FORWARD TO

1.   1.

2.   2.

3.   3.

TO DAY'S SCHEDULE

WHAT WOULD MAKE TO DAY GREAT?

HOW CAN I SET MYSELF FOR SUCCESS TO DAY?

HOW DO I WANT TO FEEL AT THE END OF TODAY?

TODAY'S AFFIRMATION   /   /

"

"

3 THINGS I'LL ACCOMPLISH TODAY   3 THINGS I LOOK FORWARD TO

1.   1.

2.   2.

3.   3.

TO DAY'S SCHEDULE

☐
☐
☐
☐
☐
☐
☐

WHAT WOULD MAKE TO DAY GREAT?

HOW CAN I SET MYSELF FOR SUCCESS TO DAY?

HOW DO I WANT TO FEEL AT THE END OF TODAY?

TODAY'S AFFIRMATION   /   /

"

                                                    "

3 THINGS I'LL ACCOMPLISH TODAY   3 THINGS I LOOK FORWARD TO

1.   1.

2.   2.

3.   3.

TO DAY'S SCHEDULE

WHAT WOULD MAKE TO DAY GREAT?

HOW CAN I SET MYSELF FOR SUCCESS TO DAY?

HOW DO I WANT TO FEEL AT THE END OF TODAY?

TODAY'S AFFIRMATION   /   /

"

                                                                          "

3 THINGS I'LL ACCOMPLISH TODAY   **3 THINGS I LOOK FORWARD TO**

1.   1.

2.   2.

3.   3.

TO DAY'S SCHEDULE

☐
☐
☐
☐
☐
☐
☐

WHAT WOULD MAKE TO DAY GREAT?

HOW CAN I SET MYSELF FOR SUCCESS TO DAY?

HOW DO I WANT TO FEEL AT THE END OF TODAY?

GRATITUDE

TODAY'S AFFIRMATION   /   /

"

"

3 THINGS I'LL ACCOMPLISH TODAY   **3 THINGS I LOOK FORWARD TO**

1.   1.

2.   2.

3.   3.

TO DAY'S SCHEDULE

☐
☐
☐
☐

WHAT WOULD MAKE TO DAY GREAT?

HOW CAN I SET MYSELF FOR SUCCESS TO DAY?

HOW DO I WANT TO FEEL AT THE END OF TODAY?

TODAY'S AFFIRMATION   /   /

"

"

3 THINGS I'LL ACCOMPLISH TODAY

1.

2.

3.

3 THINGS I LOOK FORWARD TO

1.

2.

3.

TO DAY'S SCHEDULE

- [ ]
- [ ]
- [ ]
- [ ]
- [ ]
- [ ]
- [ ]

WHAT WOULD MAKE TO DAY GREAT?

HOW CAN I SET MYSELF FOR SUCCESS TO DAY?

HOW DO I WANT TO FEEL AT THE END OF TODAY?

TODAY'S AFFIRMATION   /   /

"

"

3 THINGS I'LL ACCOMPLISH TODAY   3 THINGS I LOOK FORWARD TO

1.   1.

2.   2.

3.   3.

TO DAY'S SCHEDULE

WHAT WOULD MAKE TO DAY GREAT?

HOW CAN I SET MYSELF FOR SUCCESS TO DAY?

HOW DO I WANT TO FEEL AT THE END OF TODAY?

TODAY'S AFFIRMATION   /   /

"

"

3 THINGS I'LL ACCOMPLISH TODAY   3 THINGS I LOOK FORWARD TO

1.   1.

2.   2.

3.   3.

TO DAY'S SCHEDULE

☐
☐
☐
☐
☐
☐
☐

WHAT WOULD MAKE TO DAY GREAT?

HOW CAN I SET MYSELF FOR SUCCESS TO DAY?

HOW DO I WANT TO FEEL AT THE END OF TODAY?

TODAY'S AFFIRMATION   /   /

"

"

3 THINGS I'LL ACCOMPLISH TODAY   3 THINGS I LOOK FORWARD TO

1.   1.

2.   2.

3.   3.

TO DAY'S SCHEDULE

WHAT WOULD MAKE TO DAY GREAT?

HOW CAN I SET MYSELF FOR SUCCESS TO DAY?

HOW DO I WANT TO FEEL AT THE END OF TODAY?

TODAY'S AFFIRMATION   /   /

"

"

3 THINGS I'LL ACCOMPLISH TODAY   3 THINGS I LOOK FORWARD TO

1.   1.

2.   2.

3.   3.

TO DAY'S SCHEDULE

☐
☐
☐
☐
☐
☐

WHAT WOULD MAKE TO DAY GREAT?

HOW CAN I SET MYSELF FOR SUCCESS TO DAY?

HOW DO I WANT TO FEEL AT THE END OF TODAY?

TODAY'S AFFIRMATION   /   /

"

                                                                                    "

3 THINGS I'LL ACCOMPLISH TODAY   **3 THINGS I LOOK FORWARD TO**

1.   1.

2.   2.

3.   3.

TO DAY'S SCHEDULE

☐

☐

☐

WHAT WOULD MAKE TO DAY GREAT?

HOW CAN I SET MYSELF FOR SUCCESS TO DAY?

HOW DO I WANT TO FEEL AT THE END OF TODAY?

TODAY'S AFFIRMATION   /   /

"

"

3 THINGS I'LL ACCOMPLISH TODAY   3 THINGS I LOOK FORWARD TO

1.   1.

2.   2.

3.   3.

TO DAY'S SCHEDULE

☐
☐
☐
☐
☐
☐

WHAT WOULD MAKE TO DAY GREAT?

HOW CAN I SET MYSELF FOR SUCCESS TO DAY?

HOW DO I WANT TO FEEL AT THE END OF TODAY?

TODAY'S AFFIRMATION   /   /

"

"

3 THINGS I'LL ACCOMPLISH TODAY   3 THINGS I LOOK FORWARD TO

1.   1.

2.   2.

3.   3.

TO DAY'S SCHEDULE

WHAT WOULD MAKE TO DAY GREAT?

HOW CAN I SET MYSELF FOR SUCCESS TO DAY?

HOW DO I WANT TO FEEL AT THE END OF TODAY?

GRATITUDE

TODAY'S AFFIRMATION   /   /

"

                                                                              "

3 THINGS I'LL ACCOMPLISH TODAY   **3 THINGS I LOOK FORWARD TO**

1. _______________________   1. _______________________

2. _______________________   2. _______________________

3. _______________________   3. _______________________

TO DAY'S SCHEDULE

☐ ____

☐ ____

☐ ____

☐ ____

☐ ____

☐ ____

☐ ____

WHAT WOULD MAKE TO DAY GREAT?

HOW CAN I SET MYSELF FOR SUCCESS TO DAY?

HOW DO I WANT TO FEEL AT THE END OF TODAY?

GRATITUDE

TODAY'S AFFIRMATION   /   /

"

"

3 THINGS I'LL ACCOMPLISH TODAY

1.

2.

3.

3 THINGS I LOOK FORWARD TO

1.

2.

3.

TO DAY'S SCHEDULE

WHAT WOULD MAKE TO DAY GREAT?

HOW CAN I SET MYSELF FOR SUCCESS TO DAY?

HOW DO I WANT TO FEEL AT THE END OF TODAY?

GRATITUDE

TODAY'S AFFIRMATION   /   /

"

"

3 THINGS I'LL ACCOMPLISH TODAY

1.

2.

3.

3 THINGS I LOOK FORWARD TO

1.

2.

3.

TO DAY'S SCHEDULE

☐
☐
☐
☐
☐
☐
☐

WHAT WOULD MAKE TO DAY GREAT?

HOW CAN I SET MYSELF FOR SUCCESS TO DAY?

HOW DO I WANT TO FEEL AT THE END OF TODAY?

TODAY'S AFFIRMATION   /   /

"

"

3 THINGS I'LL ACCOMPLISH TODAY

1.

2.

3.

3 THINGS I LOOK FORWARD TO

1.

2.

3.

TO DAY'S SCHEDULE

WHAT WOULD MAKE TO DAY GREAT?

HOW CAN I SET MYSELF FOR SUCCESS TO DAY?

HOW DO I WANT TO FEEL AT THE END OF TODAY?

TODAY'S AFFIRMATION   /   /

"

"

3 THINGS I'LL ACCOMPLISH TODAY   3 THINGS I LOOK FORWARD TO

1.   1.

2.   2.

3.   3.

TO DAY'S SCHEDULE

☐
☐
☐
☐
☐
☐
☐

WHAT WOULD MAKE TO DAY GREAT?

HOW CAN I SET MYSELF FOR SUCCESS TO DAY?

HOW DO I WANT TO FEEL AT THE END OF TODAY?

TODAY'S AFFIRMATION   /   /

"

"

3 THINGS I'LL ACCOMPLISH TODAY   3 THINGS I LOOK FORWARD TO

1.   1.

2.   2.

3.   3.

TO DAY'S SCHEDULE

WHAT WOULD MAKE TO DAY GREAT?

HOW CAN I SET MYSELF FOR SUCCESS TO DAY?

HOW DO I WANT TO FEEL AT THE END OF TODAY?

TODAY'S AFFIRMATION   /   /

"

                                                                              "

3 THINGS I'LL ACCOMPLISH TODAY   3 THINGS I LOOK FORWARD TO

1.   1.

2.   2.

3.   3.

TO DAY'S SCHEDULE

☐
☐
☐
☐
☐
☐
☐

WHAT WOULD MAKE TO DAY GREAT?

HOW CAN I SET MYSELF FOR SUCCESS TO DAY?

HOW DO I WANT TO FEEL AT THE END OF TODAY?

TODAY'S AFFIRMATION   /   /

"

                                                                              "

3 THINGS I'LL ACCOMPLISH TODAY   3 THINGS I LOOK FORWARD TO

1.   1.

2.   2.

3.   3.

TO DAY'S SCHEDULE

WHAT WOULD MAKE TO DAY GREAT?

HOW CAN I SET MYSELF FOR SUCCESS TO DAY?

HOW DO I WANT TO FEEL AT THE END OF TODAY?

GRATITUDE

TODAY'S AFFIRMATION   /   /

"

"

3 THINGS I'LL ACCOMPLISH TODAY

1.

2.

3.

3 THINGS I LOOK FORWARD TO

1.

2.

3.

TO DAY'S SCHEDULE

☐
☐
☐
☐
☐
☐
☐

WHAT WOULD MAKE TO DAY GREAT?

HOW CAN I SET MYSELF FOR SUCCESS TO DAY?

HOW DO I WANT TO FEEL AT THE END OF TODAY?

TODAY'S AFFIRMATION   /   /

"

"

3 THINGS I'LL ACCOMPLISH TODAY   3 THINGS I LOOK FORWARD TO

1.   1.

2.   2.

3.   3.

TO DAY'S SCHEDULE

WHAT WOULD MAKE TO DAY GREAT?

HOW CAN I SET MYSELF FOR SUCCESS TO DAY?

HOW DO I WANT TO FEEL AT THE END OF TODAY?

GOOD DAY START WITH

GRATITUDE

TODAY'S AFFIRMATION   /   /

"

"

3 THINGS I'LL ACCOMPLISH TODAY   3 THINGS I LOOK FORWARD TO

1.   1.

2.   2.

3.   3.

TO DAY'S SCHEDULE

☐
☐
☐
☐
☐
☐
☐

WHAT WOULD MAKE TO DAY GREAT?

HOW CAN I SET MYSELF FOR SUCCESS TO DAY?

HOW DO I WANT TO FEEL AT THE END OF TODAY?

GRATITUDE

TODAY'S AFFIRMATION   /   /

"

"

3 THINGS I'LL ACCOMPLISH TODAY   3 THINGS I LOOK FORWARD TO

1.   1.

2.   2.

3.   3.

TO DAY'S SCHEDULE

WHAT WOULD MAKE TO DAY GREAT?

HOW CAN I SET MYSELF FOR SUCCESS TO DAY?

HOW DO I WANT TO FEEL AT THE END OF TODAY?

GRATITUDE

TODAY'S AFFIRMATION   /   /

"

"

3 THINGS I'LL ACCOMPLISH TODAY   3 THINGS I LOOK FORWARD TO

1.   1.

2.   2.

3.   3.

TO DAY'S SCHEDULE

☐
☐
☐
☐
☐
☐
☐

WHAT WOULD MAKE TO DAY GREAT?

HOW CAN I SET MYSELF FOR SUCCESS TO DAY?

HOW DO I WANT TO FEEL AT THE END OF TODAY?

TODAY'S AFFIRMATION   /   /

"

                                                                    "

3 THINGS I'LL ACCOMPLISH TODAY   3 THINGS I LOOK FORWARD TO

1.   1.

2.   2.

3.   3.

TO DAY'S SCHEDULE

WHAT WOULD MAKE TO DAY GREAT?

HOW CAN I SET MYSELF FOR SUCCESS TO DAY?

HOW DO I WANT TO FEEL AT THE END OF TODAY?

GRATITUDE

TODAY'S AFFIRMATION   /   /

"

"

3 THINGS I'LL ACCOMPLISH TODAY **3 THINGS I LOOK FORWARD TO**

1.   1.

2.   2.

3.   3.

TO DAY'S SCHEDULE

☐

☐

☐

☐

☐

☐

☐

WHAT WOULD MAKE TO DAY GREAT?

HOW CAN I SET MYSELF FOR SUCCESS TO DAY?

HOW DO I WANT TO FEEL AT THE END OF TODAY?

TODAY'S AFFIRMATION   /   /

"

"

3 THINGS I'LL ACCOMPLISH TODAY   3 THINGS I LOOK FORWARD TO

1.   1.

2.   2.

3.   3.

TO DAY'S SCHEDULE

WHAT WOULD MAKE TO DAY GREAT?

HOW CAN I SET MYSELF FOR SUCCESS TO DAY?

HOW DO I WANT TO FEEL AT THE END OF TODAY?

TODAY'S AFFIRMATION   /   /

"

"

3 THINGS I'LL ACCOMPLISH TODAY   3 THINGS I LOOK FORWARD TO

1.   1.

2.   2.

3.   3.

TO DAY'S SCHEDULE

☐
☐
☐
☐
☐
☐
☐

WHAT WOULD MAKE TO DAY GREAT?

HOW CAN I SET MYSELF FOR SUCCESS TO DAY?

HOW DO I WANT TO FEEL AT THE END OF TODAY?

TODAY'S AFFIRMATION   /   /

"

                                                                        "

3 THINGS I'LL ACCOMPLISH TODAY   3 THINGS I LOOK FORWARD TO

1.   1.

2.   2.

3.   3.

TO DAY'S SCHEDULE

WHAT WOULD MAKE TO DAY GREAT?

HOW CAN I SET MYSELF FOR SUCCESS TO DAY?

HOW DO I WANT TO FEEL AT THE END OF TODAY?

TODAY'S AFFIRMATION   /   /

"

"

3 THINGS I'LL ACCOMPLISH TODAY   3 THINGS I LOOK FORWARD TO

1.   1.

2.   2.

3.   3.

TO DAY'S SCHEDULE

☐

☐

☐

☐

☐

☐

☐

WHAT WOULD MAKE TO DAY GREAT?

HOW CAN I SET MYSELF FOR SUCCESS TO DAY?

HOW DO I WANT TO FEEL AT THE END OF TODAY?

GRATITUDE

TODAY'S AFFIRMATION   /   /

"

"

3 THINGS I'LL ACCOMPLISH TODAY

1.

2.

3.

3 THINGS I LOOK FORWARD TO

1.

2.

3.

TO DAY'S SCHEDULE

☐
☐
☐
☐

WHAT WOULD MAKE TO DAY GREAT?

HOW CAN I SET MYSELF FOR SUCCESS TO DAY?

HOW DO I WANT TO FEEL AT THE END OF TODAY?

TODAY'S AFFIRMATION   /   /

"

"

3 THINGS I'LL ACCOMPLISH TODAY   **3 THINGS I LOOK FORWARD TO**

1.   1.

2.   2.

3.   3.

TO DAY'S SCHEDULE

☐
☐
☐
☐
☐
☐
☐

WHAT WOULD MAKE TO DAY GREAT?

HOW CAN I SET MYSELF FOR SUCCESS TO DAY?

HOW DO I WANT TO FEEL AT THE END OF TODAY?

GRATITUDE

TODAY'S AFFIRMATION   /   /

"

                                                                              "

3 THINGS I'LL ACCOMPLISH TODAY   3 THINGS I LOOK FORWARD TO

1.   1.

2.   2.

3.   3.

TO DAY'S SCHEDULE

WHAT WOULD MAKE TO DAY GREAT?

HOW CAN I SET MYSELF FOR SUCCESS TO DAY?

HOW DO I WANT TO FEEL AT THE END OF TODAY?

TODAY'S AFFIRMATION   /   /

"

                                                                    "

3 THINGS I'LL ACCOMPLISH TODAY   **3 THINGS I LOOK FORWARD TO**

1.   1.

2.   2.

3.   3.

TO DAY'S SCHEDULE

☐
☐
☐
☐
☐
☐
☐

WHAT WOULD MAKE TO DAY GREAT?

HOW CAN I SET MYSELF FOR SUCCESS TO DAY?

HOW DO I WANT TO FEEL AT THE END OF TODAY?

GRATITUDE

TODAY'S AFFIRMATION   /   /

"

"

3 THINGS I'LL ACCOMPLISH TODAY

1.

2.

3.

3 THINGS I LOOK FORWARD TO

1.

2.

3.

TO DAY'S SCHEDULE

WHAT WOULD MAKE TO DAY GREAT?

HOW CAN I SET MYSELF FOR SUCCESS TO DAY?

HOW DO I WANT TO FEEL AT THE END OF TODAY?

GRATITUDE

TODAY'S AFFIRMATION   /   /

"

                                                                          "

3 THINGS I'LL ACCOMPLISH TODAY   **3 THINGS I LOOK FORWARD TO**

1.   1.

2.   2.

3.   3.

TO DAY'S SCHEDULE

☐
☐
☐
☐
☐
☐
☐

WHAT WOULD MAKE TO DAY GREAT?

HOW CAN I SET MYSELF FOR SUCCESS TO DAY?

HOW DO I WANT TO FEEL AT THE END OF TODAY?

TODAY'S AFFIRMATION   /   /

"

"

3 THINGS I'LL ACCOMPLISH TODAY

1.

2.

3.

3 THINGS I LOOK FORWARD TO

1.

2.

3.

TO DAY'S SCHEDULE

WHAT WOULD MAKE TO DAY GREAT?

HOW CAN I SET MYSELF FOR SUCCESS TO DAY?

HOW DO I WANT TO FEEL AT THE END OF TODAY?

GRATITUDE

TODAY'S AFFIRMATION   /   /

"

"

3 THINGS I'LL ACCOMPLISH TODAY   **3 THINGS I LOOK FORWARD TO**

1.   1.

2.   2.

3.   3.

TO DAY'S SCHEDULE

- ☐
- ☐
- ☐
- ☐
- ☐
- ☐
- ☐

WHAT WOULD MAKE TO DAY GREAT?

HOW CAN I SET MYSELF FOR SUCCESS TO DAY?

HOW DO I WANT TO FEEL AT THE END OF TODAY?

GRATITUDE

TODAY'S AFFIRMATION   /   /

"

"

3 THINGS I'LL ACCOMPLISH TODAY   3 THINGS I LOOK FORWARD TO

1.   1.

2.   2.

3.   3.

TO DAY'S SCHEDULE

☐

☐

☐

☐

☐

☐

WHAT WOULD MAKE TO DAY GREAT?

HOW CAN I SET MYSELF FOR SUCCESS TO DAY?

HOW DO I WANT TO FEEL AT THE END OF TODAY?

TODAY'S AFFIRMATION   /   /

"

"

3 THINGS I'LL ACCOMPLISH TODAY   3 THINGS I LOOK FORWARD TO

1.   1.

2.   2.

3.   3.

TO DAY'S SCHEDULE

☐
☐
☐
☐
☐
☐
☐

WHAT WOULD MAKE TO DAY GREAT?

HOW CAN I SET MYSELF FOR SUCCESS TO DAY?

HOW DO I WANT TO FEEL AT THE END OF TODAY?

TODAY'S AFFIRMATION   /   /

"

                                                                        "

3 THINGS I'LL ACCOMPLISH TODAY   3 THINGS I LOOK FORWARD TO

1.   1.

2.   2.

3.   3.

TO DAY'S SCHEDULE

WHAT WOULD MAKE TO DAY GREAT?

HOW CAN I SET MYSELF FOR SUCCESS TO DAY?

HOW DO I WANT TO FEEL AT THE END OF TODAY?

GRATITUDE

TODAY'S AFFIRMATION   /   /

"

"

3 THINGS I'LL ACCOMPLISH TODAY   **3 THINGS I LOOK FORWARD TO**

1.   1.

2.   2.

3.   3.

TO DAY'S SCHEDULE

☐
☐
☐
☐
☐
☐
☐

WHAT WOULD MAKE TO DAY GREAT?

HOW CAN I SET MYSELF FOR SUCCESS TO DAY?

HOW DO I WANT TO FEEL AT THE END OF TODAY?

GRATITUDE

TODAY'S AFFIRMATION   /   /

"

                                                                                            "

3 THINGS I'LL ACCOMPLISH TODAY   3 THINGS I LOOK FORWARD TO

1.   1.

2.   2.

3.   3.

TO DAY'S SCHEDULE

WHAT WOULD MAKE TO DAY GREAT?

HOW CAN I SET MYSELF FOR SUCCESS TO DAY?

HOW DO I WANT TO FEEL AT THE END OF TODAY?

GRATITUDE

TODAY'S AFFIRMATION   /   /

"

"

3 THINGS I'LL ACCOMPLISH TODAY

1.

2.

3.

3 THINGS I LOOK FORWARD TO

1.

2.

3.

TO DAY'S SCHEDULE

☐
☐
☐
☐
☐
☐
☐

WHAT WOULD MAKE TO DAY GREAT?

HOW CAN I SET MYSELF FOR SUCCESS TO DAY?

HOW DO I WANT TO FEEL AT THE END OF TODAY?

TODAY'S AFFIRMATION   /   /

"

"

3 THINGS I'LL ACCOMPLISH TODAY   3 THINGS I LOOK FORWARD TO

1.   1.

2.   2.

3.   3.

TO DAY'S SCHEDULE

WHAT WOULD MAKE TO DAY GREAT?

HOW CAN I SET MYSELF FOR SUCCESS TO DAY?

HOW DO I WANT TO FEEL AT THE END OF TODAY?

GRATITUDE

TODAY'S AFFIRMATION   /   /

"

"

3 THINGS I'LL ACCOMPLISH TODAY

1.

2.

3.

3 THINGS I LOOK FORWARD TO

1.

2.

3.

TO DAY'S SCHEDULE

☐
☐
☐
☐
☐
☐
☐

WHAT WOULD MAKE TO DAY GREAT?

HOW CAN I SET MYSELF FOR SUCCESS TO DAY?

HOW DO I WANT TO FEEL AT THE END OF TODAY?

TODAY'S AFFIRMATION   /   /

"

"

3 THINGS I'LL ACCOMPLISH TODAY   3 THINGS I LOOK FORWARD TO

1.   1.

2.   2.

3.   3.

TO DAY'S SCHEDULE

WHAT WOULD MAKE TO DAY GREAT?

HOW CAN I SET MYSELF FOR SUCCESS TO DAY?

HOW DO I WANT TO FEEL AT THE END OF TODAY?

TODAY'S AFFIRMATION   /   /

"

"

3 THINGS I'LL ACCOMPLISH TODAY

1.

2.

3.

3 THINGS I LOOK FORWARD TO

1.

2.

3.

TO DAY'S SCHEDULE

☐
☐
☐
☐
☐
☐
☐

WHAT WOULD MAKE TO DAY GREAT?

HOW CAN I SET MYSELF FOR SUCCESS TO DAY?

HOW DO I WANT TO FEEL AT THE END OF TODAY?

TODAY'S AFFIRMATION   /   /

"

"

3 THINGS I'LL ACCOMPLISH TODAY   3 THINGS I LOOK FORWARD TO

1.   1.

2.   2.

3.   3.

TO DAY'S SCHEDULE

WHAT WOULD MAKE TO DAY GREAT?

HOW CAN I SET MYSELF FOR SUCCESS TO DAY?

HOW DO I WANT TO FEEL AT THE END OF TODAY?

GRATITUDE

TODAY'S AFFIRMATION   /   /

"

"

3 THINGS I'LL ACCOMPLISH TODAY   3 THINGS I LOOK FORWARD TO

1.   1.

2.   2.

3.   3.

TO DAY'S SCHEDULE

☐
☐
☐
☐
☐
☐
☐

WHAT WOULD MAKE TO DAY GREAT?

HOW CAN I SET MYSELF FOR SUCCESS TO DAY?

HOW DO I WANT TO FEEL AT THE END OF TODAY?

GRATITUDE

TODAY'S AFFIRMATION　　　　　　　　　　　　　　　　/　　　　　　　/

"

"

3 THINGS I'LL ACCOMPLISH TODAY

1.

2.

3.

3 THINGS I LOOK FORWARD TO

1.

2.

3.

TO DAY'S SCHEDULE

☐
☐
☐
☐
☐
☐

WHAT WOULD MAKE TO DAY GREAT?

HOW CAN I SET MYSELF FOR SUCCESS TO DAY?

HOW DO I WANT TO FEEL AT THE END OF TODAY?

GRATITUDE

TODAY'S AFFIRMATION   /   /

"

"

3 THINGS I'LL ACCOMPLISH TODAY   3 THINGS I LOOK FORWARD TO

1.   1.

2.   2.

3.   3.

TO DAY'S SCHEDULE

☐
☐
☐
☐
☐
☐
☐

WHAT WOULD MAKE TO DAY GREAT?

HOW CAN I SET MYSELF FOR SUCCESS TO DAY?

HOW DO I WANT TO FEEL AT THE END OF TODAY?

TODAY'S AFFIRMATION   /   /

"

"

3 THINGS I'LL ACCOMPLISH TODAY   3 THINGS I LOOK FORWARD TO

1.   1.

2.   2.

3.   3.

TO DAY'S SCHEDULE

WHAT WOULD MAKE TO DAY GREAT?

HOW CAN I SET MYSELF FOR SUCCESS TO DAY?

HOW DO I WANT TO FEEL AT THE END OF TODAY?

TODAY'S AFFIRMATION ______________ / ____ / ____

"

"

3 THINGS I'LL ACCOMPLISH TODAY

1.

2.

3.

3 THINGS I LOOK FORWARD TO

1.

2.

3.

TO DAY'S SCHEDULE

- [ ]
- [ ]
- [ ]
- [ ]
- [ ]
- [ ]

WHAT WOULD MAKE TO DAY GREAT?

HOW CAN I SET MYSELF FOR SUCCESS TO DAY?

HOW DO I WANT TO FEEL AT THE END OF TODAY?

TODAY'S AFFIRMATION   /   /

"

"

3 THINGS I'LL ACCOMPLISH TODAY   3 THINGS I LOOK FORWARD TO

1.   1.

2.   2.

3.   3.

TO DAY'S SCHEDULE

☐
☐
☐
☐

WHAT WOULD MAKE TO DAY GREAT?

HOW CAN I SET MYSELF FOR SUCCESS TO DAY?

HOW DO I WANT TO FEEL AT THE END OF TODAY?

GOOD DAY START WITH

GRATITUDE

TODAY'S AFFIRMATION   /   /

"

"

3 THINGS I'LL ACCOMPLISH TODAY   3 THINGS I LOOK FORWARD TO

1.   1.

2.   2.

3.   3.

TO DAY'S SCHEDULE

☐
☐
☐
☐
☐
☐
☐

WHAT WOULD MAKE TO DAY GREAT?

HOW CAN I SET MYSELF FOR SUCCESS TO DAY?

HOW DO I WANT TO FEEL AT THE END OF TODAY?

TODAY'S AFFIRMATION   /   /

"

"

3 THINGS I'LL ACCOMPLISH TODAY

1.

2.

3.

3 THINGS I LOOK FORWARD TO

1.

2.

3.

TO DAY'S SCHEDULE

WHAT WOULD MAKE TO DAY GREAT?

HOW CAN I SET MYSELF FOR SUCCESS TO DAY?

HOW DO I WANT TO FEEL AT THE END OF TODAY?

TODAY'S AFFIRMATION   /   /

"

"

3 THINGS I'LL ACCOMPLISH TODAY   3 THINGS I LOOK FORWARD TO

1.   1.

2.   2.

3.   3.

TO DAY'S SCHEDULE

☐
☐
☐
☐
☐
☐
☐

WHAT WOULD MAKE TO DAY GREAT?

HOW CAN I SET MYSELF FOR SUCCESS TO DAY?

HOW DO I WANT TO FEEL AT THE END OF TODAY?

GRATITUDE

TODAY'S AFFIRMATION   /   /

"

"

3 THINGS I'LL ACCOMPLISH TODAY   3 THINGS I LOOK FORWARD TO

1.   1.

2.   2.

3.   3.

TO DAY'S SCHEDULE

WHAT WOULD MAKE TO DAY GREAT?

HOW CAN I SET MYSELF FOR SUCCESS TO DAY?

HOW DO I WANT TO FEEL AT THE END OF TODAY?

TODAY'S AFFIRMATION   /   /

"

"

3 THINGS I'LL ACCOMPLISH TODAY

1.

2.

3.

3 THINGS I LOOK FORWARD TO

1.

2.

3.

TO DAY'S SCHEDULE

☐
☐
☐
☐
☐
☐
☐

WHAT WOULD MAKE TO DAY GREAT?

HOW CAN I SET MYSELF FOR SUCCESS TO DAY?

HOW DO I WANT TO FEEL AT THE END OF TODAY?

GRATITUDE

TODAY'S AFFIRMATION   /   /

"

"

3 THINGS I'LL ACCOMPLISH TODAY

1.

2.

3.

3 THINGS I LOOK FORWARD TO

1.

2.

3.

TO DAY'S SCHEDULE

WHAT WOULD MAKE TO DAY GREAT?

HOW CAN I SET MYSELF FOR SUCCESS TO DAY?

HOW DO I WANT TO FEEL AT THE END OF TODAY?

GRATITUDE

TODAY'S AFFIRMATION   /   /

"

"

3 THINGS I'LL ACCOMPLISH TODAY   **3 THINGS I LOOK FORWARD TO**

1.   1.

2.   2.

3.   3.

TO DAY'S SCHEDULE

☐
☐
☐
☐
☐
☐
☐

WHAT WOULD MAKE TO DAY GREAT?

HOW CAN I SET MYSELF FOR SUCCESS TO DAY?

HOW DO I WANT TO FEEL AT THE END OF TODAY?

GOOD DAY START WITH

GRATITUDE

TODAY'S AFFIRMATION   /   /

"

"

3 THINGS I'LL ACCOMPLISH TODAY   3 THINGS I LOOK FORWARD TO

1.   1.

2.   2.

3.   3.

TO DAY'S SCHEDULE

WHAT WOULD MAKE TO DAY GREAT?

HOW CAN I SET MYSELF FOR SUCCESS TO DAY?

HOW DO I WANT TO FEEL AT THE END OF TODAY?

TODAY'S AFFIRMATION   /   /

"

                                                                    "

3 THINGS I'LL ACCOMPLISH TODAY   3 THINGS I LOOK FORWARD TO

1.   1.

2.   2.

3.   3.

TO DAY'S SCHEDULE

☐
☐
☐
☐
☐
☐
☐

WHAT WOULD MAKE TO DAY GREAT?

HOW CAN I SET MYSELF FOR SUCCESS TO DAY?

HOW DO I WANT TO FEEL AT THE END OF TODAY?

TODAY'S AFFIRMATION   /   /

"

"

3 THINGS I'LL ACCOMPLISH TODAY   3 THINGS I LOOK FORWARD TO

1.   1.

2.   2.

3.   3.

TO DAY'S SCHEDULE

WHAT WOULD MAKE TO DAY GREAT?

HOW CAN I SET MYSELF FOR SUCCESS TO DAY?

HOW DO I WANT TO FEEL AT THE END OF TODAY?

TODAY'S AFFIRMATION   /   /

"

                                                                        "

3 THINGS I'LL ACCOMPLISH TODAY   3 THINGS I LOOK FORWARD TO

1.   1.

2.   2.

3.   3.

TO DAY'S SCHEDULE

☐
☐
☐
☐
☐
☐
☐

WHAT WOULD MAKE TO DAY GREAT?

HOW CAN I SET MYSELF FOR SUCCESS TO DAY?

HOW DO I WANT TO FEEL AT THE END OF TODAY?

GOOD DAY START WITH

GRATITUDE

TODAY'S AFFIRMATION   /   /

"

"

3 THINGS I'LL ACCOMPLISH TODAY

1.

2.

3.

3 THINGS I LOOK FORWARD TO

1.

2.

3.

TO DAY'S SCHEDULE

☐

☐

☐

☐

WHAT WOULD MAKE TO DAY GREAT?

HOW CAN I SET MYSELF FOR SUCCESS TO DAY?

HOW DO I WANT TO FEEL AT THE END OF TODAY?

TODAY'S AFFIRMATION   /   /

"

"

3 THINGS I'LL ACCOMPLISH TODAY   3 THINGS I LOOK FORWARD TO

1.   1.

2.   2.

3.   3.

TO DAY'S SCHEDULE

☐
☐
☐
☐
☐
☐

WHAT WOULD MAKE TO DAY GREAT?

HOW CAN I SET MYSELF FOR SUCCESS TO DAY?

HOW DO I WANT TO FEEL AT THE END OF TODAY?

TODAY'S AFFIRMATION   /   /

"

"

3 THINGS I'LL ACCOMPLISH TODAY   3 THINGS I LOOK FORWARD TO

1.   1.

2.   2.

3.   3.

TO DAY'S SCHEDULE

WHAT WOULD MAKE TO DAY GREAT?

HOW CAN I SET MYSELF FOR SUCCESS TO DAY?

HOW DO I WANT TO FEEL AT THE END OF TODAY?

TODAY'S AFFIRMATION   /   /

"

"

3 THINGS I'LL ACCOMPLISH TODAY   3 THINGS I LOOK FORWARD TO

1.   1.

2.   2.

3.   3.

TO DAY'S SCHEDULE

☐
☐
☐
☐
☐
☐
☐

WHAT WOULD MAKE TO DAY GREAT?

HOW CAN I SET MYSELF FOR SUCCESS TO DAY?

HOW DO I WANT TO FEEL AT THE END OF TODAY?

TODAY'S AFFIRMATION   /   /

"

"

3 THINGS I'LL ACCOMPLISH TODAY   3 THINGS I LOOK FORWARD TO

1.   1.

2.   2.

3.   3.

TO DAY'S SCHEDULE

WHAT WOULD MAKE TO DAY GREAT?

HOW CAN I SET MYSELF FOR SUCCESS TO DAY?

HOW DO I WANT TO FEEL AT THE END OF TODAY?

TODAY'S AFFIRMATION   /   /

"

"

3 THINGS I'LL ACCOMPLISH TODAY   3 THINGS I LOOK FORWARD TO

1.   1.

2.   2.

3.   3.

TO DAY'S SCHEDULE

☐
☐
☐
☐
☐
☐
☐

WHAT WOULD MAKE TO DAY GREAT?

HOW CAN I SET MYSELF FOR SUCCESS TO DAY?

HOW DO I WANT TO FEEL AT THE END OF TODAY?

TODAY'S AFFIRMATION   /   /

"

                                                                    "

3 THINGS I'LL ACCOMPLISH TODAY   3 THINGS I LOOK FORWARD TO

1.   1.

2.   2.

3.   3.

TO DAY'S SCHEDULE

WHAT WOULD MAKE TO DAY GREAT?

HOW CAN I SET MYSELF FOR SUCCESS TO DAY?

HOW DO I WANT TO FEEL AT THE END OF TODAY?

GRATITUDE

TODAY'S AFFIRMATION   /   /

"

"

3 THINGS I'LL ACCOMPLISH TODAY

1.

2.

3.

3 THINGS I LOOK FORWARD TO

1.

2.

3.

TO DAY'S SCHEDULE

☐
☐
☐
☐
☐
☐
☐

WHAT WOULD MAKE TO DAY GREAT?

HOW CAN I SET MYSELF FOR SUCCESS TO DAY?

HOW DO I WANT TO FEEL AT THE END OF TODAY?

TODAY'S AFFIRMATION   /   /

"

"

3 THINGS I'LL ACCOMPLISH TODAY   3 THINGS I LOOK FORWARD TO

1.   1.

2.   2.

3.   3.

TO DAY'S SCHEDULE

WHAT WOULD MAKE TO DAY GREAT?

HOW CAN I SET MYSELF FOR SUCCESS TO DAY?

HOW DO I WANT TO FEEL AT THE END OF TODAY?

GRATITUDE

TODAY'S AFFIRMATION   /   /

"

"

3 THINGS I'LL ACCOMPLISH TODAY

1.

2.

3.

3 THINGS I LOOK FORWARD TO

1.

2.

3.

TO DAY'S SCHEDULE

- [ ]
- [ ]
- [ ]
- [ ]
- [ ]
- [ ]
- [ ]

WHAT WOULD MAKE TO DAY GREAT?

HOW CAN I SET MYSELF FOR SUCCESS TO DAY?

HOW DO I WANT TO FEEL AT THE END OF TODAY?

GRATITUDE

TODAY'S AFFIRMATION ___________ / _______ / _______

"

"

3 THINGS I'LL ACCOMPLISH TODAY

1. ___________________________

2. ___________________________

3. ___________________________

3 THINGS I LOOK FORWARD TO

1. ___________________________

2. ___________________________

3. ___________________________

TO DAY'S SCHEDULE

☐ _______________________________

☐ _______________________________

☐ _______________________________

WHAT WOULD MAKE TO DAY GREAT?

HOW CAN I SET MYSELF FOR SUCCESS TO DAY?

HOW DO I WANT TO FEEL AT THE END OF TODAY?

TODAY'S AFFIRMATION   /   /

"

"

3 THINGS I'LL ACCOMPLISH TODAY   3 THINGS I LOOK FORWARD TO

1.   1.

2.   2.

3.   3.

TO DAY'S SCHEDULE

- [ ]
- [ ]
- [ ]
- [ ]
- [ ]
- [ ]
- [ ]

WHAT WOULD MAKE TO DAY GREAT?

HOW CAN I SET MYSELF FOR SUCCESS TO DAY?

HOW DO I WANT TO FEEL AT THE END OF TODAY?

TODAY'S AFFIRMATION   /   /

"

"

3 THINGS I'LL ACCOMPLISH TODAY   3 THINGS I LOOK FORWARD TO

1.   1.

2.   2.

3.   3.

TO DAY'S SCHEDULE

☐
☐
☐
☐

WHAT WOULD MAKE TO DAY GREAT?

HOW CAN I SET MYSELF FOR SUCCESS TO DAY?

HOW DO I WANT TO FEEL AT THE END OF TODAY?

GRATITUDE

TODAY'S AFFIRMATION   /   /

"

"

3 THINGS I'LL ACCOMPLISH TODAY   3 THINGS I LOOK FORWARD TO

1.   1.

2.   2.

3.   3.

TO DAY'S SCHEDULE

☐
☐
☐
☐
☐
☐
☐

WHAT WOULD MAKE TO DAY GREAT?

HOW CAN I SET MYSELF FOR SUCCESS TO DAY?

HOW DO I WANT TO FEEL AT THE END OF TODAY?

GRATITUDE

TODAY'S AFFIRMATION   /   /

"

"

3 THINGS I'LL ACCOMPLISH TODAY

1.

2.

3.

3 THINGS I LOOK FORWARD TO

1.

2.

3.

TO DAY'S SCHEDULE

☐

☐

☐

WHAT WOULD MAKE TO DAY GREAT?

HOW CAN I SET MYSELF FOR SUCCESS TO DAY?

HOW DO I WANT TO FEEL AT THE END OF TODAY?

GRATITUDE

TODAY'S AFFIRMATION   /   /

"

"

3 THINGS I'LL ACCOMPLISH TODAY

1.

2.

3.

3 THINGS I LOOK FORWARD TO

1.

2.

3.

TO DAY'S SCHEDULE

☐
☐
☐
☐
☐
☐
☐

WHAT WOULD MAKE TO DAY GREAT?

HOW CAN I SET MYSELF FOR SUCCESS TO DAY?

HOW DO I WANT TO FEEL AT THE END OF TODAY?

GRATITUDE

TODAY'S AFFIRMATION   /   /

"

"

3 THINGS I'LL ACCOMPLISH TODAY   3 THINGS I LOOK FORWARD TO

1.   1.

2.   2.

3.   3.

TO DAY'S SCHEDULE

WHAT WOULD MAKE TO DAY GREAT?

HOW CAN I SET MYSELF FOR SUCCESS TO DAY?

HOW DO I WANT TO FEEL AT THE END OF TODAY?

GOOD DAY START WITH

GRATITUDE

TODAY'S AFFIRMATION   /   /

"

"

3 THINGS I'LL ACCOMPLISH TODAY   3 THINGS I LOOK FORWARD TO

1.   1.

2.   2.

3.   3.

TO DAY'S SCHEDULE

WHAT WOULD MAKE TO DAY GREAT?

HOW CAN I SET MYSELF FOR SUCCESS TO DAY?

HOW DO I WANT TO FEEL AT THE END OF TODAY?

TODAY'S AFFIRMATION   /   /

"

"

3 THINGS I'LL ACCOMPLISH TODAY

1.

2.

3.

3 THINGS I LOOK FORWARD TO

1.

2.

3.

TO DAY'S SCHEDULE

WHAT WOULD MAKE TO DAY GREAT?

HOW CAN I SET MYSELF FOR SUCCESS TO DAY?

HOW DO I WANT TO FEEL AT THE END OF TODAY?

TODAY'S AFFIRMATION   /   /

"

                                                                                "

3 THINGS I'LL ACCOMPLISH TODAY   3 THINGS I LOOK FORWARD TO

1.   1.

2.   2.

3.   3.

TO DAY'S SCHEDULE

☐
☐
☐
☐
☐
☐
☐

WHAT WOULD MAKE TO DAY GREAT?

HOW CAN I SET MYSELF FOR SUCCESS TO DAY?

HOW DO I WANT TO FEEL AT THE END OF TODAY?

TODAY'S AFFIRMATION   /   /

"

"

3 THINGS I'LL ACCOMPLISH TODAY   3 THINGS I LOOK FORWARD TO

1.   1.

2.   2.

3.   3.

TO DAY'S SCHEDULE

WHAT WOULD MAKE TO DAY GREAT?

HOW CAN I SET MYSELF FOR SUCCESS TO DAY?

HOW DO I WANT TO FEEL AT THE END OF TODAY?

TODAY'S AFFIRMATION   /   /

"

"

3 THINGS I'LL ACCOMPLISH TODAY   3 THINGS I LOOK FORWARD TO

1.   1.

2.   2.

3.   3.

TO DAY'S SCHEDULE

☐
☐
☐
☐
☐
☐

WHAT WOULD MAKE TO DAY GREAT?

HOW CAN I SET MYSELF FOR SUCCESS TO DAY?

HOW DO I WANT TO FEEL AT THE END OF TODAY?

TODAY'S AFFIRMATION   /   /

"

                                                                                    "

3 THINGS I'LL ACCOMPLISH TODAY   3 THINGS I LOOK FORWARD TO

1.   1.

2.   2.

3.   3.

TO DAY'S SCHEDULE

WHAT WOULD MAKE TO DAY GREAT?

HOW CAN I SET MYSELF FOR SUCCESS TO DAY?

HOW DO I WANT TO FEEL AT THE END OF TODAY?

TODAY'S AFFIRMATION   /   /

"

"

3 THINGS I'LL ACCOMPLISH TODAY   3 THINGS I LOOK FORWARD TO

1.   1.

2.   2.

3.   3.

TO DAY'S SCHEDULE

☐
☐
☐
☐
☐
☐
☐

WHAT WOULD MAKE TO DAY GREAT?

HOW CAN I SET MYSELF FOR SUCCESS TO DAY?

HOW DO I WANT TO FEEL AT THE END OF TODAY?

GRATITUDE

TODAY'S AFFIRMATION   /   /

"

"

3 THINGS I'LL ACCOMPLISH TODAY

1.

2.

3.

3 THINGS I LOOK FORWARD TO

1.

2.

3.

TO DAY'S SCHEDULE

WHAT WOULD MAKE TO DAY GREAT?

HOW CAN I SET MYSELF FOR SUCCESS TO DAY?

HOW DO I WANT TO FEEL AT THE END OF TODAY?

TODAY'S AFFIRMATION   /   /

"

"

3 THINGS I'LL ACCOMPLISH TODAY

1.

2.

3.

3 THINGS I LOOK FORWARD TO

1.

2.

3.

TO DAY'S SCHEDULE

- [ ]
- [ ]
- [ ]
- [ ]
- [ ]
- [ ]
- [ ]

WHAT WOULD MAKE TO DAY GREAT?

HOW CAN I SET MYSELF FOR SUCCESS TO DAY?

HOW DO I WANT TO FEEL AT THE END OF TODAY?

TODAY'S AFFIRMATION   /   /

"

                                                                    "

3 THINGS I'LL ACCOMPLISH TODAY   3 THINGS I LOOK FORWARD TO

1.   1.

2.   2.

3.   3.

TO DAY'S SCHEDULE

WHAT WOULD MAKE TO DAY GREAT?

HOW CAN I SET MYSELF FOR SUCCESS TO DAY?

HOW DO I WANT TO FEEL AT THE END OF TODAY?

TODAY'S AFFIRMATION   /   /

"

"

3 THINGS I'LL ACCOMPLISH TODAY   **3 THINGS I LOOK FORWARD TO**

1.   1.

2.   2.

3.   3.

TO DAY'S SCHEDULE

☐
☐
☐
☐
☐
☐
☐

WHAT WOULD MAKE TO DAY GREAT?

HOW CAN I SET MYSELF FOR SUCCESS TO DAY?

HOW DO I WANT TO FEEL AT THE END OF TODAY?

GRATITUDE

TODAY'S AFFIRMATION   /   /

"

"

3 THINGS I'LL ACCOMPLISH TODAY   **3 THINGS I LOOK FORWARD TO**

1.   1.

2.   2.

3.   3.

TO DAY'S SCHEDULE

☐
☐
☐

WHAT WOULD MAKE TO DAY GREAT?

HOW CAN I SET MYSELF FOR SUCCESS TO DAY?

HOW DO I WANT TO FEEL AT THE END OF TODAY?

TODAY'S AFFIRMATION   /   /

"

                                                                              "

3 THINGS I'LL ACCOMPLISH TODAY   3 THINGS I LOOK FORWARD TO

1.   1.

2.   2.

3.   3.

TO DAY'S SCHEDULE

☐
☐
☐
☐
☐
☐

WHAT WOULD MAKE TO DAY GREAT?

HOW CAN I SET MYSELF FOR SUCCESS TO DAY?

HOW DO I WANT TO FEEL AT THE END OF TODAY?

TODAY'S AFFIRMATION   /   /

"

"

3 THINGS I'LL ACCOMPLISH TODAY   3 THINGS I LOOK FORWARD TO

1.   1.

2.   2.

3.   3.

TO DAY'S SCHEDULE

WHAT WOULD MAKE TO DAY GREAT?

HOW CAN I SET MYSELF FOR SUCCESS TO DAY?

HOW DO I WANT TO FEEL AT THE END OF TODAY?

TODAY'S AFFIRMATION   /   /

"

"

3 THINGS I'LL ACCOMPLISH TODAY

1.

2.

3.

3 THINGS I LOOK FORWARD TO

1.

2.

3.

TO DAY'S SCHEDULE

- [ ]
- [ ]
- [ ]
- [ ]
- [ ]
- [ ]
- [ ]

WHAT WOULD MAKE TO DAY GREAT?

HOW CAN I SET MYSELF FOR SUCCESS TO DAY?

HOW DO I WANT TO FEEL AT THE END OF TODAY?

GRATITUDE

TODAY'S AFFIRMATION   /   /

"

"

3 THINGS I'LL ACCOMPLISH TODAY

1.

2.

3.

3 THINGS I LOOK FORWARD TO

1.

2.

3.

TO DAY'S SCHEDULE

☐
☐
☐
☐

WHAT WOULD MAKE TO DAY GREAT?

HOW CAN I SET MYSELF FOR SUCCESS TO DAY?

HOW DO I WANT TO FEEL AT THE END OF TODAY?

GOOD DAY START WITH

GRATITUDE

TODAY'S AFFIRMATION   /   /

"

"

3 THINGS I'LL ACCOMPLISH TODAY   3 THINGS I LOOK FORWARD TO

1.   1.

2.   2.

3.   3.

TO DAY'S SCHEDULE

☐
☐
☐
☐
☐
☐

WHAT WOULD MAKE TO DAY GREAT?

HOW CAN I SET MYSELF FOR SUCCESS TO DAY?

HOW DO I WANT TO FEEL AT THE END OF TODAY?

GRATITUDE

TODAY'S AFFIRMATION   /   /

"

"

3 THINGS I'LL ACCOMPLISH TODAY

1.

2.

3.

3 THINGS I LOOK FORWARD TO

1.

2.

3.

TO DAY'S SCHEDULE

WHAT WOULD MAKE TO DAY GREAT?

HOW CAN I SET MYSELF FOR SUCCESS TO DAY?

HOW DO I WANT TO FEEL AT THE END OF TODAY?

TODAY'S AFFIRMATION   /   /

"

"

3 THINGS I'LL ACCOMPLISH TODAY   3 THINGS I LOOK FORWARD TO

1.   1.

2.   2.

3.   3.

TO DAY'S SCHEDULE

☐
☐
☐
☐
☐
☐
☐

WHAT WOULD MAKE TO DAY GREAT?

HOW CAN I SET MYSELF FOR SUCCESS TO DAY?

HOW DO I WANT TO FEEL AT THE END OF TODAY?

GRATITUDE

TODAY'S AFFIRMATION   /   /

"

"

3 THINGS I'LL ACCOMPLISH TODAY   3 THINGS I LOOK FORWARD TO

1.   1.

2.   2.

3.   3.

TO DAY'S SCHEDULE

☐
☐
☐
☐
☐

WHAT WOULD MAKE TO DAY GREAT?

HOW CAN I SET MYSELF FOR SUCCESS TO DAY?

HOW DO I WANT TO FEEL AT THE END OF TODAY?

TODAY'S AFFIRMATION   /   /

"

                                                        "

3 THINGS I'LL ACCOMPLISH TODAY   3 THINGS I LOOK FORWARD TO

1.   1.

2.   2.

3.   3.

TO DAY'S SCHEDULE

☐
☐
☐
☐
☐
☐
☐

WHAT WOULD MAKE TO DAY GREAT?

HOW CAN I SET MYSELF FOR SUCCESS TO DAY?

HOW DO I WANT TO FEEL AT THE END OF TODAY?

GRATITUDE

TODAY'S AFFIRMATION   /   /

"

"

3 THINGS I'LL ACCOMPLISH TODAY

1.

2.

3.

3 THINGS I LOOK FORWARD TO

1.

2.

3.

TO DAY'S SCHEDULE

WHAT WOULD MAKE TO DAY GREAT?

HOW CAN I SET MYSELF FOR SUCCESS TO DAY?

HOW DO I WANT TO FEEL AT THE END OF TODAY?

TODAY'S AFFIRMATION   /   /

"

"

3 THINGS I'LL ACCOMPLISH TODAY   3 THINGS I LOOK FORWARD TO

1.   1.

2.   2.

3.   3.

TO DAY'S SCHEDULE

☐
☐
☐
☐
☐
☐
☐

WHAT WOULD MAKE TO DAY GREAT?

HOW CAN I SET MYSELF FOR SUCCESS TO DAY?

HOW DO I WANT TO FEEL AT THE END OF TODAY?

TODAY'S AFFIRMATION   /   /

"

"

3 THINGS I'LL ACCOMPLISH TODAY   3 THINGS I LOOK FORWARD TO

1.   1.

2.   2.

3.   3.

TO DAY'S SCHEDULE

WHAT WOULD MAKE TO DAY GREAT?

HOW CAN I SET MYSELF FOR SUCCESS TO DAY?

HOW DO I WANT TO FEEL AT THE END OF TODAY?

TODAY'S AFFIRMATION   /   /

"

                                                                    "

3 THINGS I'LL ACCOMPLISH TODAY   3 THINGS I LOOK FORWARD TO

1.   1.

2.   2.

3.   3.

TO DAY'S SCHEDULE

☐
☐
☐
☐
☐
☐

WHAT WOULD MAKE TO DAY GREAT?

HOW CAN I SET MYSELF FOR SUCCESS TO DAY?

HOW DO I WANT TO FEEL AT THE END OF TODAY?

TODAY'S AFFIRMATION   /   /

"

"

3 THINGS I'LL ACCOMPLISH TODAY

1.

2.

3.

3 THINGS I LOOK FORWARD TO

1.

2.

3.

TO DAY'S SCHEDULE

WHAT WOULD MAKE TO DAY GREAT?

HOW CAN I SET MYSELF FOR SUCCESS TO DAY?

HOW DO I WANT TO FEEL AT THE END OF TODAY?

GRATITUDE

TODAY'S AFFIRMATION   /   /

"

"

3 THINGS I'LL ACCOMPLISH TODAY   **3 THINGS I LOOK FORWARD TO**

1.   1.

2.   2.

3.   3.

TO DAY'S SCHEDULE

☐
☐
☐
☐
☐
☐
☐

WHAT WOULD MAKE TO DAY GREAT?

HOW CAN I SET MYSELF FOR SUCCESS TO DAY?

HOW DO I WANT TO FEEL AT THE END OF TODAY?

GRATITUDE

TODAY'S AFFIRMATION   /   /

"

"

3 THINGS I'LL ACCOMPLISH TODAY   3 THINGS I LOOK FORWARD TO

1.   1.

2.   2.

3.   3.

TO DAY'S SCHEDULE

WHAT WOULD MAKE TO DAY GREAT?

HOW CAN I SET MYSELF FOR SUCCESS TO DAY?

HOW DO I WANT TO FEEL AT THE END OF TODAY?

TODAY'S AFFIRMATION   /   /

"

"

3 THINGS I'LL ACCOMPLISH TODAY

1.

2.

3.

3 THINGS I LOOK FORWARD TO

1.

2.

3.

TO DAY'S SCHEDULE

- [ ]
- [ ]
- [ ]
- [ ]
- [ ]
- [ ]
- [ ]

WHAT WOULD MAKE TO DAY GREAT?

HOW CAN I SET MYSELF FOR SUCCESS TO DAY?

HOW DO I WANT TO FEEL AT THE END OF TODAY?

TODAY'S AFFIRMATION   /   /

"

"

3 THINGS I'LL ACCOMPLISH TODAY   3 THINGS I LOOK FORWARD TO

1.   1.

2.   2.

3.   3.

TO DAY'S SCHEDULE

WHAT WOULD MAKE TO DAY GREAT?

HOW CAN I SET MYSELF FOR SUCCESS TO DAY?

HOW DO I WANT TO FEEL AT THE END OF TODAY?

TODAY'S AFFIRMATION   /   /

"

                                                                              "

3 THINGS I'LL ACCOMPLISH TODAY   3 THINGS I LOOK FORWARD TO

1.   1.

2.   2.

3.   3.

TO DAY'S SCHEDULE

☐
☐
☐
☐
☐
☐
☐

WHAT WOULD MAKE TO DAY GREAT?

HOW CAN I SET MYSELF FOR SUCCESS TO DAY?

HOW DO I WANT TO FEEL AT THE END OF TODAY?

TODAY'S AFFIRMATION   /   /

"

"

3 THINGS I'LL ACCOMPLISH TODAY

1.

2.

3.

3 THINGS I LOOK FORWARD TO

1.

2.

3.

TO DAY'S SCHEDULE

WHAT WOULD MAKE TO DAY GREAT?

HOW CAN I SET MYSELF FOR SUCCESS TO DAY?

HOW DO I WANT TO FEEL AT THE END OF TODAY?

TODAY'S AFFIRMATION   /   /

"

"

3 THINGS I'LL ACCOMPLISH TODAY   3 THINGS I LOOK FORWARD TO

1.   1.

2.   2.

3.   3.

TO DAY'S SCHEDULE

☐
☐
☐
☐
☐
☐
☐

WHAT WOULD MAKE TO DAY GREAT?

HOW CAN I SET MYSELF FOR SUCCESS TO DAY?

HOW DO I WANT TO FEEL AT THE END OF TODAY?

TODAY'S AFFIRMATION   /   /

"

"

3 THINGS I'LL ACCOMPLISH TODAY   3 THINGS I LOOK FORWARD TO

1.   1.

2.   2.

3.   3.

TO DAY'S SCHEDULE

WHAT WOULD MAKE TO DAY GREAT?

HOW CAN I SET MYSELF FOR SUCCESS TO DAY?

HOW DO I WANT TO FEEL AT THE END OF TODAY?

GRATITUDE

TODAY'S AFFIRMATION   /   /

"

"

3 THINGS I'LL ACCOMPLISH TODAY   3 THINGS I LOOK FORWARD TO

1.   1.

2.   2.

3.   3.

TO DAY'S SCHEDULE

- [ ]
- [ ]
- [ ]
- [ ]
- [ ]
- [ ]
- [ ]

WHAT WOULD MAKE TO DAY GREAT?

HOW CAN I SET MYSELF FOR SUCCESS TO DAY?

HOW DO I WANT TO FEEL AT THE END OF TODAY?

GRATITUDE

TODAY'S AFFIRMATION   /   /

"

"

3 THINGS I'LL ACCOMPLISH TODAY   3 THINGS I LOOK FORWARD TO

1.   1.

2.   2.

3.   3.

TO DAY'S SCHEDULE

☐
☐
☐
☐

WHAT WOULD MAKE TO DAY GREAT?

HOW CAN I SET MYSELF FOR SUCCESS TO DAY?

HOW DO I WANT TO FEEL AT THE END OF TODAY?

TODAY'S AFFIRMATION   /   /

"

                                                                              "

3 THINGS I'LL ACCOMPLISH TODAY   3 THINGS I LOOK FORWARD TO

1.   1.

2.   2.

3.   3.

TO DAY'S SCHEDULE

☐
☐
☐
☐
☐
☐
☐

WHAT WOULD MAKE TO DAY GREAT?

HOW CAN I SET MYSELF FOR SUCCESS TO DAY?

HOW DO I WANT TO FEEL AT THE END OF TODAY?

GRATITUDE

TODAY'S AFFIRMATION .... / .... / ....

"

"

3 THINGS I'LL ACCOMPLISH TODAY

1.

2.

3.

3 THINGS I LOOK FORWARD TO

1.

2.

3.

TO DAY'S SCHEDULE

WHAT WOULD MAKE TO DAY GREAT?

HOW CAN I SET MYSELF FOR SUCCESS TO DAY?

HOW DO I WANT TO FEEL AT THE END OF TODAY?

TODAY'S AFFIRMATION   /   /

"

"

3 THINGS I'LL ACCOMPLISH TODAY   **3 THINGS I LOOK FORWARD TO**

1.   1.

2.   2.

3.   3.

TO DAY'S SCHEDULE

☐
☐
☐
☐
☐
☐
☐

WHAT WOULD MAKE TO DAY GREAT?

HOW CAN I SET MYSELF FOR SUCCESS TO DAY?

HOW DO I WANT TO FEEL AT THE END OF TODAY?

TODAY'S AFFIRMATION   /   /

"

"

3 THINGS I'LL ACCOMPLISH TODAY | 3 THINGS I LOOK FORWARD TO

1.   1.

2.   2.

3.   3.

TO DAY'S SCHEDULE

WHAT WOULD MAKE TO DAY GREAT?

HOW CAN I SET MYSELF FOR SUCCESS TO DAY?

HOW DO I WANT TO FEEL AT THE END OF TODAY?

TODAY'S AFFIRMATION   /   /

"

"

3 THINGS I'LL ACCOMPLISH TODAY   3 THINGS I LOOK FORWARD TO

1.   1.

2.   2.

3.   3.

TO DAY'S SCHEDULE

☐
☐
☐
☐
☐
☐
☐

WHAT WOULD MAKE TO DAY GREAT?

HOW CAN I SET MYSELF FOR SUCCESS TO DAY?

HOW DO I WANT TO FEEL AT THE END OF TODAY?

TODAY'S AFFIRMATION   /   /

"

"

3 THINGS I'LL ACCOMPLISH TODAY   3 THINGS I LOOK FORWARD TO

1.   1.

2.   2.

3.   3.

TO DAY'S SCHEDULE

WHAT WOULD MAKE TO DAY GREAT?

HOW CAN I SET MYSELF FOR SUCCESS TO DAY?

HOW DO I WANT TO FEEL AT THE END OF TODAY?

TODAY'S AFFIRMATION   /   /

"

"

3 THINGS I'LL ACCOMPLISH TODAY   3 THINGS I LOOK FORWARD TO

1.   1.

2.   2.

3.   3.

TO DAY'S SCHEDULE

☐
☐
☐
☐
☐
☐
☐

WHAT WOULD MAKE TO DAY GREAT?

HOW CAN I SET MYSELF FOR SUCCESS TO DAY?

HOW DO I WANT TO FEEL AT THE END OF TODAY?

TODAY'S AFFIRMATION   /   /

"

"

3 THINGS I'LL ACCOMPLISH TODAY   3 THINGS I LOOK FORWARD TO

1.   1.

2.   2.

3.   3.

TO DAY'S SCHEDULE

WHAT WOULD MAKE TO DAY GREAT?

HOW CAN I SET MYSELF FOR SUCCESS TO DAY?

HOW DO I WANT TO FEEL AT THE END OF TODAY?

GOOD DAY START WITH

GRATITUDE

TODAY'S AFFIRMATION   /   /

"

"

3 THINGS I'LL ACCOMPLISH TODAY **3 THINGS I LOOK FORWARD TO**

1.   1.

2.   2.

3.   3.

TO DAY'S SCHEDULE

- [ ]
- [ ]
- [ ]
- [ ]
- [ ]
- [ ]
- [ ]

WHAT WOULD MAKE TO DAY GREAT?

HOW CAN I SET MYSELF FOR SUCCESS TO DAY?

HOW DO I WANT TO FEEL AT THE END OF TODAY?

TODAY'S AFFIRMATION   /   /

"

"

3 THINGS I'LL ACCOMPLISH TODAY   3 THINGS I LOOK FORWARD TO

1.   1.

2.   2.

3.   3.

TO DAY'S SCHEDULE

WHAT WOULD MAKE TO DAY GREAT?

HOW CAN I SET MYSELF FOR SUCCESS TO DAY?

HOW DO I WANT TO FEEL AT THE END OF TODAY?

TODAY'S AFFIRMATION   /   /

"

"

3 THINGS I'LL ACCOMPLISH TODAY   3 THINGS I LOOK FORWARD TO

1.   1.

2.   2.

3.   3.

TO DAY'S SCHEDULE

☐
☐
☐
☐
☐
☐
☐

WHAT WOULD MAKE TO DAY GREAT?

HOW CAN I SET MYSELF FOR SUCCESS TO DAY?

HOW DO I WANT TO FEEL AT THE END OF TODAY?

GRATITUDE

TODAY'S AFFIRMATION   /   /

"

"

3 THINGS I'LL ACCOMPLISH TODAY

1.

2.

3.

3 THINGS I LOOK FORWARD TO

1.

2.

3.

TO DAY'S SCHEDULE

WHAT WOULD MAKE TO DAY GREAT?

HOW CAN I SET MYSELF FOR SUCCESS TO DAY?

HOW DO I WANT TO FEEL AT THE END OF TODAY?

GOOD DAY START WITH
GRATITUDE

TODAY'S AFFIRMATION   /   /

"

"

3 THINGS I'LL ACCOMPLISH TODAY   **3 THINGS I LOOK FORWARD TO**

1.   1.

2.   2.

3.   3.

TO DAY'S SCHEDULE

☐
☐
☐
☐
☐
☐
☐

WHAT WOULD MAKE TO DAY GREAT?

HOW CAN I SET MYSELF FOR SUCCESS TO DAY?

HOW DO I WANT TO FEEL AT THE END OF TODAY?

GOOD DAY START WITH

GRATITUDE

TODAY'S AFFIRMATION   /   /

"

"

3 THINGS I'LL ACCOMPLISH TODAY

1.

2.

3.

3 THINGS I LOOK FORWARD TO

1.

2.

3.

TO DAY'S SCHEDULE

WHAT WOULD MAKE TO DAY GREAT?

HOW CAN I SET MYSELF FOR SUCCESS TO DAY?

HOW DO I WANT TO FEEL AT THE END OF TODAY?

GRATITUDE

TODAY'S AFFIRMATION   /   /

"

"

3 THINGS I'LL ACCOMPLISH TODAY   **3 THINGS I LOOK FORWARD TO**

1.   1.

2.   2.

3.   3.

TO DAY'S SCHEDULE

- [ ]
- [ ]
- [ ]
- [ ]
- [ ]
- [ ]
- [ ]

WHAT WOULD MAKE TO DAY GREAT?

HOW CAN I SET MYSELF FOR SUCCESS TO DAY?

HOW DO I WANT TO FEEL AT THE END OF TODAY?

TODAY'S AFFIRMATION   /   /

    "

                                                            "

3 THINGS I'LL ACCOMPLISH TODAY   3 THINGS I LOOK FORWARD TO

1.   1.

2.   2.

3.   3.

TO DAY'S SCHEDULE

WHAT WOULD MAKE TO DAY GREAT?

HOW CAN I SET MYSELF FOR SUCCESS TO DAY?

HOW DO I WANT TO FEEL AT THE END OF TODAY?

GRATITUDE

TODAY'S AFFIRMATION   /   /

"

"

3 THINGS I'LL ACCOMPLISH TODAY

1.

2.

3.

3 THINGS I LOOK FORWARD TO

1.

2.

3.

TO DAY'S SCHEDULE

☐

☐

☐

☐

☐

☐

☐

WHAT WOULD MAKE TO DAY GREAT?

HOW CAN I SET MYSELF FOR SUCCESS TO DAY?

HOW DO I WANT TO FEEL AT THE END OF TODAY?

TODAY'S AFFIRMATION   /   /

"

"

3 THINGS I'LL ACCOMPLISH TODAY   3 THINGS I LOOK FORWARD TO

1.   1.

2.   2.

3.   3.

TO DAY'S SCHEDULE

WHAT WOULD MAKE TO DAY GREAT?

HOW CAN I SET MYSELF FOR SUCCESS TO DAY?

HOW DO I WANT TO FEEL AT THE END OF TODAY?

TODAY'S AFFIRMATION   /   /

"

"

3 THINGS I'LL ACCOMPLISH TODAY   3 THINGS I LOOK FORWARD TO

1.   1.

2.   2.

3.   3.

TO DAY'S SCHEDULE

☐
☐
☐
☐
☐
☐
☐

WHAT WOULD MAKE TO DAY GREAT?

HOW CAN I SET MYSELF FOR SUCCESS TO DAY?

HOW DO I WANT TO FEEL AT THE END OF TODAY?

TODAY'S AFFIRMATION   /   /

"

"

3 THINGS I'LL ACCOMPLISH TODAY

1.

2.

3.

3 THINGS I LOOK FORWARD TO

1.

2.

3.

TO DAY'S SCHEDULE

WHAT WOULD MAKE TO DAY GREAT?

HOW CAN I SET MYSELF FOR SUCCESS TO DAY?

HOW DO I WANT TO FEEL AT THE END OF TODAY?

TODAY'S AFFIRMATION   /   /

"

"

3 THINGS I'LL ACCOMPLISH TODAY   3 THINGS I LOOK FORWARD TO

1.   1.

2.   2.

3.   3.

TO DAY'S SCHEDULE

☐
☐
☐
☐
☐
☐
☐

WHAT WOULD MAKE TO DAY GREAT?

HOW CAN I SET MYSELF FOR SUCCESS TO DAY?

HOW DO I WANT TO FEEL AT THE END OF TODAY?

TODAY'S AFFIRMATION   /   /

"

"

3 THINGS I'LL ACCOMPLISH TODAY   3 THINGS I LOOK FORWARD TO

1.   1.

2.   2.

3.   3.

TO DAY'S SCHEDULE

WHAT WOULD MAKE TO DAY GREAT?

HOW CAN I SET MYSELF FOR SUCCESS TO DAY?

HOW DO I WANT TO FEEL AT THE END OF TODAY?

GOOD DAY START WITH

GRATITUDE

TODAY'S AFFIRMATION   /   /

"

"

3 THINGS I'LL ACCOMPLISH TODAY	3 THINGS I LOOK FORWARD TO
1.	1.
2.	2.
3.	3.

TO DAY'S SCHEDULE

☐
☐
☐
☐
☐
☐
☐

WHAT WOULD MAKE TO DAY GREAT?

HOW CAN I SET MYSELF FOR SUCCESS TO DAY?

HOW DO I WANT TO FEEL AT THE END OF TODAY?

GOOD DAY START WITH

GRATITUDE

TODAY'S AFFIRMATION   /   /

"

"

3 THINGS I'LL ACCOMPLISH TODAY   3 THINGS I LOOK FORWARD TO

1.   1.

2.   2.

3.   3.

TO DAY'S SCHEDULE

WHAT WOULD MAKE TO DAY GREAT?

HOW CAN I SET MYSELF FOR SUCCESS TO DAY?

HOW DO I WANT TO FEEL AT THE END OF TODAY?

GRATITUDE

TODAY'S AFFIRMATION   /   /

"

"

3 THINGS I'LL ACCOMPLISH TODAY   3 THINGS I LOOK FORWARD TO

1.   1.

2.   2.

3.   3.

TO DAY'S SCHEDULE

☐
☐
☐
☐
☐
☐
☐

WHAT WOULD MAKE TO DAY GREAT?

HOW CAN I SET MYSELF FOR SUCCESS TO DAY?

HOW DO I WANT TO FEEL AT THE END OF TODAY?

GRATITUDE

TODAY'S AFFIRMATION   /   /

"

"

3 THINGS I'LL ACCOMPLISH TODAY

1.

2.

3.

3 THINGS I LOOK FORWARD TO

1.

2.

3.

TO DAY'S SCHEDULE

WHAT WOULD MAKE TO DAY GREAT?

HOW CAN I SET MYSELF FOR SUCCESS TO DAY?

HOW DO I WANT TO FEEL AT THE END OF TODAY?

TODAY'S AFFIRMATION   /   /

"

"

3 THINGS I'LL ACCOMPLISH TODAY   3 THINGS I LOOK FORWARD TO

1.   1.

2.   2.

3.   3.

TO DAY'S SCHEDULE

☐
☐
☐
☐
☐
☐
☐

WHAT WOULD MAKE TO DAY GREAT?

HOW CAN I SET MYSELF FOR SUCCESS TO DAY?

HOW DO I WANT TO FEEL AT THE END OF TODAY?

GRATITUDE

TODAY'S AFFIRMATION   /   /

"

"

3 THINGS I'LL ACCOMPLISH TODAY   **3 THINGS I LOOK FORWARD TO**

1.   1.

2.   2.

3.   3.

TO DAY'S SCHEDULE

WHAT WOULD MAKE TO DAY GREAT?

HOW CAN I SET MYSELF FOR SUCCESS TO DAY?

HOW DO I WANT TO FEEL AT THE END OF TODAY?

GOOD DAY START WITH

GRATITUDE

TODAY'S AFFIRMATION   /   /

"

"

3 THINGS I'LL ACCOMPLISH TODAY   **3 THINGS I LOOK FORWARD TO**

1.   1.

2.   2.

3.   3.

TO DAY'S SCHEDULE

☐
☐
☐
☐
☐
☐
☐

WHAT WOULD MAKE TO DAY GREAT?

HOW CAN I SET MYSELF FOR SUCCESS TO DAY?

HOW DO I WANT TO FEEL AT THE END OF TODAY?

TODAY'S AFFIRMATION   /   / .

"

"

3 THINGS I'LL ACCOMPLISH TODAY

1.

2.

3.

3 THINGS I LOOK FORWARD TO

1.

2.

3.

TO DAY'S SCHEDULE

WHAT WOULD MAKE TO DAY GREAT?

HOW CAN I SET MYSELF FOR SUCCESS TO DAY?

HOW DO I WANT TO FEEL AT THE END OF TODAY?

TODAY'S AFFIRMATION   /   /

"

3 THINGS I'LL ACCOMPLISH TODAY   3 THINGS I LOOK FORWARD TO

1.   1.

2.   2.

3.   3.

TO DAY'S SCHEDULE

☐
☐
☐
☐
☐
☐
☐

WHAT WOULD MAKE TO DAY GREAT?

HOW CAN I SET MYSELF FOR SUCCESS TO DAY?

HOW DO I WANT TO FEEL AT THE END OF TODAY?

TODAY'S AFFIRMATION   /   /

"

"

3 THINGS I'LL ACCOMPLISH TODAY   3 THINGS I LOOK FORWARD TO

1.   1.

2.   2.

3.   3.

TO DAY'S SCHEDULE

WHAT WOULD MAKE TO DAY GREAT?

HOW CAN I SET MYSELF FOR SUCCESS TO DAY?

HOW DO I WANT TO FEEL AT THE END OF TODAY?

GOOD DAY START WITH
GRATITUDE

TODAY'S AFFIRMATION   /   /

"

                                                                    "

3 THINGS I'LL ACCOMPLISH TODAY   **3 THINGS I LOOK FORWARD TO**

1.   1.

2.   2.

3.   3.

TO DAY'S SCHEDULE

☐
☐
☐
☐
☐
☐
☐

WHAT WOULD MAKE TO DAY GREAT?

HOW CAN I SET MYSELF FOR SUCCESS TO DAY?

HOW DO I WANT TO FEEL AT THE END OF TODAY?

TODAY'S AFFIRMATION   /   /

"

"

3 THINGS I'LL ACCOMPLISH TODAY   3 THINGS I LOOK FORWARD TO

1.   1.

2.   2.

3.   3.

TO DAY'S SCHEDULE

WHAT WOULD MAKE TO DAY GREAT?

HOW CAN I SET MYSELF FOR SUCCESS TO DAY?

HOW DO I WANT TO FEEL AT THE END OF TODAY?

GOOD DAY START WITH
GRATITUDE

TODAY'S AFFIRMATION   /   /

"

"

3 THINGS I'LL ACCOMPLISH TODAY   3 THINGS I LOOK FORWARD TO

1.   1.

2.   2.

3.   3.

TO DAY'S SCHEDULE

☐
☐
☐
☐
☐
☐
☐

WHAT WOULD MAKE TO DAY GREAT?

HOW CAN I SET MYSELF FOR SUCCESS TO DAY?

HOW DO I WANT TO FEEL AT THE END OF TODAY?

TODAY'S AFFIRMATION   /   /

"

"

3 THINGS I'LL ACCOMPLISH TODAY   **3 THINGS I LOOK FORWARD TO**

1.   1.

2.   2.

3.   3.

TO DAY'S SCHEDULE

WHAT WOULD MAKE TO DAY GREAT?

HOW CAN I SET MYSELF FOR SUCCESS TO DAY?

HOW DO I WANT TO FEEL AT THE END OF TODAY?

TODAY'S AFFIRMATION   /   /

"

"

3 THINGS I'LL ACCOMPLISH TODAY

1.

2.

3.

3 THINGS I LOOK FORWARD TO

1.

2.

3.

TO DAY'S SCHEDULE

WHAT WOULD MAKE TO DAY GREAT?

HOW CAN I SET MYSELF FOR SUCCESS TO DAY?

HOW DO I WANT TO FEEL AT THE END OF TODAY?

GRATITUDE

TODAY'S AFFIRMATION   /   /

"

"

3 THINGS I'LL ACCOMPLISH TODAY

1.

2.

3.

3 THINGS I LOOK FORWARD TO

1.

2.

3.

TO DAY'S SCHEDULE

WHAT WOULD MAKE TO DAY GREAT?

HOW CAN I SET MYSELF FOR SUCCESS TO DAY?

HOW DO I WANT TO FEEL AT THE END OF TODAY?

TODAY'S AFFIRMATION   /   /

"

"

3 THINGS I'LL ACCOMPLISH TODAY

1.

2.

3.

3 THINGS I LOOK FORWARD TO

1.

2.

3.

TO DAY'S SCHEDULE

☐
☐
☐
☐
☐
☐
☐

WHAT WOULD MAKE TO DAY GREAT?

HOW CAN I SET MYSELF FOR SUCCESS TO DAY?

HOW DO I WANT TO FEEL AT THE END OF TODAY?

GRATITUDE

TODAY'S AFFIRMATION   /   /

"

"

3 THINGS I'LL ACCOMPLISH TODAY

1.

2.

3.

3 THINGS I LOOK FORWARD TO

1.

2.

3.

TO DAY'S SCHEDULE

WHAT WOULD MAKE TO DAY GREAT?

HOW CAN I SET MYSELF FOR SUCCESS TO DAY?

HOW DO I WANT TO FEEL AT THE END OF TODAY?